MINISTRY PROTOCOL

Let all things be done decently and in order.

DIEGO MESA

Largo, MD

Copyright © 2020 Diego Mesa

All rights reserved under international copyright law. No part of this book may be reproduced or transmitted in any form or by any means, electronic or mechanical, including photocopying, recording, or by any information storage and retrieval system, without the express, written permission of the publisher or the author. The exception is reviewers, who may quote brief passages in a review.

Christian Living Books, Inc.
P. O. Box 7584
Largo, MD 20792
christianlivingbooks.com
We bring your dreams to fruition.

ISBN 9781562292096

All Scripture quotations are taken from the New King James Version®. Copyright © 1982 by Thomas Nelson. Used by permission. All rights reserved.

CONTENTS

Introduction v

Chapter 1 – Ministry Protocol is Biblical 9

Chapter 2 – The Purpose of Ministry Protocol. 15

Chapter 3 – Personal Conduct 19

Chapter 4 – Church Conduct 41

Chapter 5 – Responsibilities to the Church and Members 57

Chapter 6 – Accountability in Relationships. 71

Chapter 7 – Leadership 83

Chapter 8 – Spiritual Maturity in the Gifts. 89

About the Author 105

INTRODUCTION

WHAT WOULD AVIATION be without protocol? Are there protocols on your job, at the gym?

What would the military be without protocol? How can you have a marriage without it? Is there a protocol to pass laws? Is there protocol enforced by police officers when someone is arrested?

The term protocol is defined as a code of policies and procedural standards established by an organization whether secular or religious, to provide purpose, direction, and guidelines with the ultimate objective of maintaining and sustaining order. The need for a book that provides guidelines on how this concept applies to the church is the impetus for this book, *Ministry Protocol*.

Ministry Protocol is a compilation based on many years of pastoral experience. Issues that are rarely discussed, yet pondered by many, are examined in this book. Observations of repeated and innumerable errors made by the composite of the body of Christ cultivated in my heart an urgent need to address these issues. The mandate to be obedient, exercise common sense and walk in God's wisdom is imperative and must be taught and learned. *Ministry Protocol* is an attempt to provide the tools and knowledge necessary to keep people from sinning, prevent church splits, discourage people from leaving their God-given assignments, and to help churches mature in God.

Challenges are inevitable within a church; only the recently saved or the uninvolved are immune. The tenets presented in *Ministry Protocol* will eliminate the prevalent utilization of excuses generated and supported by ignorance or misinformation. Protocol, properly developed and implemented, will positively impact and reduce the number of individuals who can inadvertently cause strife, confusion, division and headache.

It is hoped that in reading *Ministry Protocol*, church members can enjoy improved interpersonal relationships and acquire or exercise understanding, accountability and responsibility. For the church to be productive with optimum output, unwavering direction coupled with a unified purpose must be in place. The examples and suggestions made in this book are merely illustrative and are not exhaustive. Protocol is equal to doing all things in an orderly fashion and not being out of order.

To function successfully in most situations, it is important to be fully aware of the organizational purpose, direction, vision, destination, guidelines, policies, boundaries or parameters. The objective of church protocol is not to control our lives, but to protect lives. By analogy, speed limit laws are enacted to increase road safety. The ramification of reduced traffic fatalities is undeniable. The laws are not randomly instituted to control our lives. With the enactment of speed laws, a comprehensive study is conducted to determine safe speeds based on location and environmental factors. Unfortunately, so many times the Bible, God's law, is misunderstood. The prevalent belief becomes that God is trying to control our lives. God is trying to protect us, not exercise dominion and control.

It may be contended that the twenty-first-century church is weak because it is out of order. Many problems, errors, and frustrations have occurred within the church because of misunderstandings, misinterpretations, negligence, ignorance, and naiveté. The underlying reason that the conditions above exist is a lack of adherence to protocol. So many people have left the church hurt, offended, and angry simply because they lacked knowledge of church protocol which could have rendered clarity and made the inexplicable explicable. Moreover, conditions frequently exist in churches where protocol may be existent but is not properly communicated.

Luke 12:48 reads, "For everyone to whom much is given, from him much will be required." This teaching is not to be exclusively retained for "us four and no more"; it is to be shared. I am presenting the resources, information and wisdom shared in *Ministry Protocol* to do my part in winning souls and tearing down the kingdom of darkness. I want more for the church. I strongly sense that the message contained herein can be a blessing to the Body of Christ.

Ministry Protocol is intended to be a reference document—a manual, if you will—that will shape our character as we, as members of His church, constantly seek to reflect the will of Jesus Christ. The tenets of ethical conduct are intended to provide guidance and rules of accountability for the church. Abundant Living Family Church (AFLC) strives to maintain high standards for the ministry. We want to be an available resource to the Body of Christ, accepting and exemplifying the principles of protocol. May you enjoy the journey as we examine how God does things decently and in order – with excellence, structure, methods and rules. I believe Christians can function better in the Body of Christ when we honor and respect God's protocols. From us to Him and from us to one another. Sometimes we can be quicker to understand protocol in the business world or outside of church but can be ignorant or arrogant to and within the Kingdom of God, church, and Body of Christ.

CHAPTER 1

MINISTRY PROTOCOL IS BIBLICAL

> *For God is not the author of confusion but of peace, as in all the churches of the saints. Let all things be done decently and in order.* (1 Corinthians 14:33, 40)

IN EXAMINING THE Old Testament, God's sense of order is readily discernible. Everything in the temple or sanctuary was built in an orderly manner. When Noah built the Ark, he followed God's prescribed specifications of exact square footage and type of wood to use in the construction. When Jesus fed the 5,000, He told the people to be seated in fifties and hundreds. Everything God does is done decently and in order... not loosey-goosey.

The church, which is comprised of each one of us individually and collectively as believers, must be in order. When our lives are out of order, our witness, power, and strength are out of order. In the church, ministry protocol provides the structure needed to ensure compliance with His Word that "all things be done decently and in order." Ministry protocol is biblical. Esther could not enter the King's presence without it, and Boaz had to follow protocol to marry Ruth. Psalm 100:4 tells us how to enter God's presence. Psalm 66:14 tells us how to experience answered prayer.

"Everything is to be done decently and in order" includes, but is not limited to, the Kingdom of God, our personal lives, and church ethics. The query may be that if we live spiritual lives and pray, won't God take care of the rest? If we live our lives in chaos, the Lord cannot bless us regardless of how much we pray, how many times we fall out (an expression, Pentecostalism) in the Holy Spirit, how often we speak in tongues, shout, or dance. When our lives are inconsistent with the Word of God, brothers and sisters, we are wasting our prayers. Those who steadfastly believe that they are redeemed and exempt from the boundaries and standards established by God are being deceived. There are no exceptions. The command is clear—a life that glorifies God is one where everything is done decently and in order.

A balanced life is an inherent component of an orderly life. In the church, ministry protocol can provide the system needed to supply the order we need. Nevertheless, we all have families, friends and jobs where the absence of a God mandated lifestyle can result in chaos. We must avoid being drawn into the extremes of life. We can shout, dance, have a Spirit-filled Pentecostal service where we speak in tongues and move in the Gifts of the Spirit. Then, to unequivocally sustain a balanced life, we need to go home and treat our spouses well, share in family time, pay our bills, live moral and ethical lives, and go out and serve, love, give, and witness. A life that epitomizes order will have balance. That's a 360-degree life that's lived right, not in part or portion which is like having a diet coke with chocolate cake.

1 Corinthians 14:33 states, "God is not the author of confusion but of peace, as in all the churches of the saints." This verse applies to all church denominations; therefore, no church is exempt from the command of God. Furthermore, if there are no saints in the church, there will be chaos and confusion.

True Christ-followers will not precipitate confusion but promote order.

> *Dishonest scales are an abomination to the Lord, but a just weight is His delight.* (Proverbs 11:1)

This verse refers to a false balance; a false balance is an abomination to Him. There are Christians who can pray, but they can't get along well with others. There are Christians who can quote every Bible Scripture, but they are gossipers and complainers. Note the imbalance in these lives. God wants us to excel and grow in all areas of our lives and not just in areas that we find easy or fun or where we feel comfortable. God wants us to address those areas that deal with the "ex's" in our lives—the ex-spouse, ex-boss, ex-pastor—that cause us to be resentful, bitter, or unforgiving. There are those who attend church every Sunday and enjoy the Spirit of God, but then walk out and express hate toward friends, family and loved ones. This truly exemplifies "dishonest scales." A hypocritical life preaches one thing but purposefully lives something different.

A balanced life provides protection from the devil and reveals that the devil is not as powerful as many Christians may believe. The Book of Revelation reveals that when we finally see the devil, we will be amazed that he had the power to torment nations and bring them to their knees. The question becomes: Was the devil really that powerful, or was it our disobedience, disorderly actions, double standards, and lack of respect toward God that empowered him?

There are some Christians who are very resistant to order. Disorder can't be ignored or condoned. Many people today are not unlike those of the Corinthian church. They need strong direction. They need to submit to the strength and attitude of someone like Titus who made it clear. Titus, a Gentile, was Paul's companion and was extremely instrumental in Paul's ministry. During Paul's first missionary trip, Titus was saved. He was a troubleshooter who was direct and brutally honest. However, he always prayed for each person whom he admonished to live an orderly life.

In contrast to Titus, Timothy was a young, loving and gentle pastor. When Timothy was sent to the Corinthian church, he was unable to pastor the people who were aggressive, controlling, and domineering... and not about to listen to Timothy! These people needed a Titus; Paul sent Titus there to set the church in order. The need for order in the Corinthian church is recounted in 1 Corinthians 3. For our purpose, it is sufficient to say it was a carnal church which excelled in gifts, but there was no fruit. For example, someone had a successful business but was still lacking. Another was extremely gifted (anointed) but had character weaknesses.

Paul writes to Titus what can be described as a prescription for the level of order we must strive to achieve:

> *But as for you, speak the things which are proper for sound doctrine: that the older men be sober, reverent, temperate, sound in faith, in love, in patience; the older women likewise, that they be reverent in behavior, not slanderers, not given to much wine, teachers of good things that they admonish the young women to love their husbands, to love their children, to be discreet, chaste, homemakers, good, obedient to their own husbands, that the word of God may not be blasphemed. Likewise, exhort the young men to be sober-minded, in all things showing yourself to be a pattern of good works; in doctrine showing integrity, reverence, incorruptibility; sound speech that cannot be condemned, that one who is an opponent may be ashamed, having nothing evil to say of you.* (Titus 2:1-8)

Powerful! What a witness for the Lord! The precepts described above are not only to be used when interacting with members of the body of Christ but in all facets of our lives and in every relationship. The verse continues:

> *Exhort bondservants to be obedient to their own masters to be well pleasing in all things, not answering back, not pilfering, but showing all good fidelity, that they may adorn the doctrine of God our Savior in all things. For the grace of God that brings salvation has appeared to all*

> *men, teaching us that denying ungodliness and worldly lusts, we should live soberly, righteously, and godly in the present age.* (Titus 2:9-12)

There are innumerable examples that can be cited to underscore and support what we already know: the basis for protocol or prescribed order is biblical. Obedience to His Word is the key to achieving the life He wants for each and every one of us.

KEY TRUTH

Always remember that God gives us the Word to teach us how to live a life decently and in order. Be obedient and choose to change those areas of life that the Holy Spirit reveals are out of order. Remember obedience is better than sacrifice. No one can live out of order–abusing, following trends, fads, or false doctrine–as well as obey and follow the Holy Scriptures. It's when we put down the Word of God and get caught up in feelings-driven messages and imbalanced leadership that we get hurt and into error. Judge everything by the Word of God and the Spirit of God, not by how something looks or feels to you. Remember that nobody likes a bathroom, gas pump, or vending machine that is out of order!

CHAPTER 2

THE PURPOSE OF MINISTRY PROTOCOL

For this reason I left you in Crete, that you should set in order the things that are lacking, and appoint elders in every city as I commanded you. (Titus 1:5)

WHEN WE GET our lives together, watch out! When our lives are in order then we will witness the miracles of God! People always ask, "Where are the miracles?

Where is the outpouring? Where is the power?" God's throne room is wide open to us, but because our lives are sometimes out of order, we are not in a position to receive or experience the miracles, outpouring and power. We are in a position of resistance.

There will always be someone who will make the statement, "Well, we've been redeemed from the curse of the law, and I don't believe that there should be structure in the body of Christ. I just believe we ought to simply flow and let things happen." This perspective is not biblical. It cannot be reiterated enough... let everything be done decently and in order in the conduct of our marriage, homes, jobs, finances, pleasure and leisures. What is the purpose of the Word of God but to give us structure and boundaries? If not, God would say, "Just pray to me, and I'll tell you what to do." He already did that! He gave us His Word to tell us what to do. That doesn't mean we should not pray. We ought to pray, but don't neglect God's Word.

When we purchase new items, particularly those that require assembly, the instructions are always in the box; yet how many of us follow those instructions? For example, one Christmas we bought our boys an electric scooter. Believe it or not, I actually read the instructions… I find that the older I get, the more I read the directions. The directions described potential problems and instructions on how to troubleshoot a malfunctioning battery or brake line. These instructions gave me guidelines and directions. If I had failed to read the instructions, the time needed to assemble that scooter could have been greatly increased. Moreover, our boys' safety could have been compromised by riding a scooter that had been unsafely or improperly assembled. Do you consistently fail to read and follow God's assembly instructions: the Holy Bible? Judge, test, examine and evaluate everything by the Scripture, every deed, action, intent, thought and decision. Everywhere we go, there are guidelines. When we go to the gym, are there not guidelines? Dripping perspiration all over the machines without wiping them down after use is strictly prohibited. Wherever we go, we see signs that provide instruction and direction. Imagine the chaos that would result in our communities if there were no signs, directions, signal lights, or lane markers.

Within the church today, direction is desperately needed regarding ministry protocol. If we do not understand how to operate in our calling, ministries, and churches, how can we ever prevail against the attacks of the enemy when we step out to be used by God in ministry? Understanding the "why" of ministry protocol will determine "how" things will be done within the church. The "why" is the motive, intent, reason, and purpose. Why? What is the purpose of the church, pastor, offering, or building?

We, as Christians, must learn to understand the purpose of God's order within the ministry and our personal lives. Order is not meant to control our lives as much as it is to protect our lives and keep unnecessary heartache from happening. When we learn and understand the purpose of God's order we will begin to see the miracles, (blessings, favor, and healings) and the outpourings of God manifest from the spiritual realm into the natural realm. Godly outcomes and Godly results are what we all want.

> Judge, test, examine and evaluate everything by the Scripture.

Our personal conduct can negatively impact our lives within the ministry. Thus far, we have examined the biblical basis and purpose of ministry protocol. In Chapter 3, guidelines and practical suggestions on personal conduct are delineated.

The words of Paul to Titus come to mind:

> *In all things showing yourself to be a pattern of good works; in doctrine showing integrity, reverence, incorruptibility.* (Titus 2:7)

KEY TRUTH

Remember the anointing, gifts, abilities and talents only take you so far. Character, integrity, and discipline take you the rest of the way. Also, being successful in some areas of life is no excuse to ignore challenges or weaknesses in other areas of life. Let's not let our ignored character flaws become someone's stumbling block for coming or committing to Jesus.

CHAPTER 3

PERSONAL CONDUCT

Let every soul be subject to the governing authorities. For there is no authority except from God, and the authorities that exist are appointed by God. Therefore, whoever resists the authority resists the ordinance of God and those who resist will bring judgment on themselves. For rulers are not terrors to good works, but to evil. Do you want to be unafraid of the authority? Do what is good, and you will have praise from the same. For he is God's minister to you for good. But if you do evil, be afraid; for he does not bear the sword in vain; for he is God's minister, an avenger to execute wrath on him who practices evil. Therefore, you must be subject, not only because of wrath but also for conscience sake. For because of this you also pay taxes, for they are God's ministers attending continually to this very thing. Render therefore to all their due: taxes to whom taxes are due, customs to whom customs, fear to whom fear, honor to whom honor. (Romans 13:1-7)

AS CHRISTIANS, WE should conduct our lives in a manner that brings glory to Jesus Christ as the living head of the church. This demonstrates our faithfulness to the Gospel. Our personal conduct must always reflect a respect for the authority and ordinance of God. Our daily lives are hectic, and we frequently fail to exercise care and diligence in our actions and decision making. We just want to get things done!

If we are to experience the life that God wants for each of us, it becomes imperative that we stop and think before we engage in any behavior that is suspect or calls into question our integrity. This chapter delves into situations that each of us faces daily.

How many times have you been in places or situations where, when viewed by others, your good could have been perceived as evil or your lifestyle did not compliment or enhance the Gospel? As Christians, we are to live above reproach and care how our lives can be interpreted by others.

Being Alone with Someone of the Opposite Sex

Situations frequently occur within the church that can be the genesis of misconception, mistrust, and the appearance of evil. Being alone with someone of the opposite sex is one of those situations. Let's examine this issue within the framework of ministry protocol as it specifically applies to interpersonal relationships. To avoid negative consequences, I strongly suggest that one-on-one behind-closed-door meetings, appointments, counseling sessions, and casual conversation with someone of the opposite sex be done strictly cautionary. Make sure that your good intentions cannot be interpreted in a bad way.

Abstain from every form of evil. (1 Thessalonians 5:22)

Therefore do not let your good be spoken of as evil. (Romans 14:16)

The following scenario is illustrative of how easily good intentions can be misinterpreted and perceived as evil: It is approaching a late hour and the pastor and Sister So-and-So are observed exiting the dark and empty church building. The pastor is loved and trusted, but he just violated the Word of God (appearance of evil). He cannot blame the devil for coming in and stealing his testimony. People, who love their pastor, have now been presented with a reason to doubt the pastor's integrity and question his judgment. The pastor could have had a perfectly acceptable reason for being with Sister So-and-So, but the point is missed – the appearance of evil is present because of foolishness, nonsense, and ignorance on the part of the pastor. The Word of God has now been violated and the misguided pastor is now open to attack. He can pray for mercy and ask God to help him, but because a biblical principle was breached, he has cast a shadow of doubt and unfortunately stained his reputation. This could also apply to giving someone of the opposite sex, other than

> **Make sure that your good intentions cannot be interpreted in a bad way.**

family, a ride in your vehicle. One action could cast a negative shadow.

We are all to desist giving the appearance of evil, not just pastors, staff, elders, deacons, and church leadership. Myriad situations can be perfectly innocent, yet they violate the Word of God as stated in Romans 12:9 and 1 Thessalonians 5:22. For example, when two single people of the opposite sex are observed sitting in a parked car, what thoughts cross the minds of most? Would anyone automatically assume that the individuals are completely innocent? Once again, that is an appearance issue; innocence or guilt is not being contended. The appearance of evil is present. One must constantly be on guard. Avoid any situation where one's character can be questioned, regardless of the setting. Business professionals of both genders who work with support staff must be very mindful of their surroundings and their actions. Everyone must avoid impropriety, whether real or imagined.

It cannot be assumed that everyone will feel, think, or react the same. Caution should be used when ministering to anyone, particularly those with whom a longstanding relationship is absent. Even though from one perspective, a situation is completely devoid of any impropriety, the other person's feelings, baggage or motives are unknown. The person could be very lonely and susceptible to misinterpretation of any situation where a caring heart is present. A single incident can compromise integrity and destroy credibility because we have a heart to minister to someone who is hurting. The challenge lies in the inability to truly know all about the other person. There are lonely people out there who will misconstrue innocent statements and make assumptions with no logical basis. You say, "Hello," and they think you said, "I love you." You compliment their sweater, and their interpretation is you are asking them to take off their clothes. You ask them for a piece of gum, and they think you want to kiss them. I'm being facetious but you get the point.

Red flags should go up when someone requests a private meeting, because the issue is not really a need for privacy but possibly an improper motive. Also, be careful when people make statements that serve to create emotional attachments and feed the flesh and ego. There are a multitude of resources and people capable of assisting those in need. No one person is the only one who cares, understands, or has all the answers. I have heard too many sad stories of pastors falling into the trap of feeling they are the sole source of support and understanding for needy individuals.

When an attraction develops, whether mutual or not, radar, sirens, bells and whistles should be immediately activated and any interaction must be avoided. Self-preservation of integrity and soul dictates lockdown, red alert and protection mode: "I cannot look at you. I cannot be around you. I cannot talk to you because you are a threat or a temptation to me." Assertively address the issue. Be clear and decisive in conveying that there can be no involvement that violates God's Word. Be absolutely honest with yourself about who you are attracted to, and watch out when you are defending a person, action, or intent when a loved one or close friend confronts you. Don't defend or choose a stranger over a loved one's suggestion, remark or consideration. Today, with same-sex attraction, all the same precautions and warnings need to be in place.

KEY TRUTH

Be mindful of being alone with the opposite sex. The location is immaterial – whether indoors or outdoors – always remain in public view. Mates or friends should be present during any meeting between individuals of the opposite sex. Keep the door of your office open when meeting with the opposite sex such as colleagues and assistants. Try to conduct business during business office hours rather than schedule after-hour meetings. Try to have a third party with you for protection and accountability.

Dating Within the Church

When dating within the church, one must be cautious, sensitive, accountable, and respectful. Church is like a family. We would never want to hurt our natural brothers and sisters; the same standard should be applied to our spiritual brothers and sisters. We also must remember that we know their father – God. Dating within the church is a precarious undertaking at best; too many times, when couples attend the same church, the relationship with the church is tainted when the dating relationship fails.

No one wants to see a bunch of "ex's" when he or she attends church—that would make anyone feel uncomfortable – maybe even enough to change churches. Often, God brings people to a certain church. However, because there are wolves in sheep's clothing – also known as "players" – or just plain ignorance, people can be hurt and feel there is no other recourse but to leave. We must be wise and remember that the "wolves" are going to try to act like Christians. They will shout, just as we do, "Hallelujah! Praise the Lord!" Despite suspicion that a "player" is among our church family, we must not automatically assume the worse of any person. In due time, the true nature of their hearts will be revealed.

The "player" is not always to blame for the problems that occur when dating within the church. Frequently, women overreact and right away want to claim that man and drag him to the altar. Not so fast! These men must first be tested, evaluated, examined, and researched. This applies to both men and women.

In Acts 20:28 and 1 Peter 5:2, God tells us to know the flock. Always, seek counsel from leadership. The church leadership does not want to control anyone. However, there may be relevant information to which leadership is privy that can prevent the hurt and disappointment experienced by those who enter what may ultimately be characterized as bad relationships.

When bad relationships result, the enemy then discourages those involved from attending church. For instance, it can be disheartening to come to church only to see an "ex" with someone else. Unfortunately, in every church there are "players" – those who will take advantage of others. The havoc they create can be devastating.

This is proper ministry protocol: at the beginning of the relationship, a couple should request pastoral consultation. It's too late to seek counsel after the fiftieth date or once a wedding date has been set. Pastoral counseling becomes irrelevant at this point. The pastor or leader faces the possibility of being rebuked by the couple because the comments made by leadership may be inconsistent with decisions the couple has already made. People have a Vegas wedding, approach their pastor the next week and say, "Pastor, look what the Lord did! He blessed us." At that point, our options are limited. All we can do is continue to love our church family members.

When dating, one should be extremely wary of anyone who raises the issue of leaving the church. It is always unacceptable when someone you are dating suggests that you leave your church and begin visiting other churches. Under these circumstances, the bells and whistles should sound loudly and clearly. The moment someone says, "You know, let's start visiting other churches" is the moment the response must be, "Wait a minute. If God sent you here to me, then He would want you to worship side-by-side with me here and grow in the ministry together." The underlying reasons and rationale to begin visiting other churches must be thoroughly examined or undoubtedly the issue will fester.

There can be complicating factors to the aforementioned scenario. A woman whose boyfriend attends another church and is already established there has a predicament.

If the relationship continues and becomes serious, the woman will eventually have to leave her church unless God is dealing with the man to come to the woman's church. Attending separate churches is not an option. Conversely, if a woman has been attending a church for five years, and the man she is seeing does not regularly attend another church but recently rededicated his life to the Lord and is just visiting churches; then he may choose to come and join with the woman and become a member of her church. If the man loves the woman, he will love what the Word in her church has done for her and will want to be a part. A clear indicator of trouble exists if the man asserts any of the following: "You need to get out of that teaching. I know of a better church. Your church is always talking about responsibility, accountability, and challenging us men. I know how to take care of my business. I don't need anyone to tell me anything." Run… don't walk… away from that relationship.

A relationship with a man who wants to increase both his and his mate's church attendance is standing on a firm foundation. Many church-going women may begin to lose their walk with the Lord when their men are not interested in church. They never missed service before; then suddenly, they are consistently missing service. They are not moving forward in that relationship—they are moving backward. Both men and women should want a mate who encourages a closer relationship with the Lord and not act as a divisive factor. I have personally witnessed beautiful ladies, who were vulnerable and somewhat naïve, meeting and then getting married to an individual whose level of commitment to God was questionable. I don't know where those ladies are today. It would be wonderful if I could unequivocally state that they attend another church down the street, because I would praise God for that. However, I do know they no longer attend church at ALFC. I question whether God was really leading that relationship. Why would He bless a union where there is an imbalance? Don't allow loneliness, desperation or pressure to drive you to settle for someone where there is not compatibility... only compromise. Don't ignore the cracks in someone's character. Don't think you're different from others that have experienced hurt from the person you're dating.

I know that we are all adults; however, remember that we have a church family. We want to respect the house of God. We all need to be sensitive and never view the church as a singles' club or a pick up stop to shop for and discard women and men at will. Developing a meaningful relationship and truly exploring and getting to know a person individually is required. There are some who preach that dating within the church is not permissible. I do not subscribe to this teaching. I believe a healthy church should teach that dating can exist if people are willing to submit to the authority of sound, structured guidelines. Furthermore, there's group dating and non-physical dating (no touching) that's more so focused on maintaining a friendship.

There is no facet of life where one can function successfully without an understanding of the rules and regulations. Board games, sports, not to mention most daily activities – require that the rules be clearly comprehended; otherwise, the activity would be meaningless with no way to measure achievement, success, failure or outcomes.

As previously discussed, the church is not in the dating game business where we openly condone any and all behavior simply because those involved are consenting adults. At ALFC, if leadership begins to see people who are hurting as a result of improper behavior, we confront the offending party. When dating, ensure that everything is done decently and in order, giving no appearance of evil. Specifically, there should be no touching and physical intimacy resulting in strong emotional and physical ties.

Getting to know someone requires time. My recommendation is the implementation of a morning, afternoon, and night dating program to keep the emotions, pressure of romance and temptation at bay:

- Morning dating occurs during an introductory period where only the best of each person is revealed. This phase is rather superficial but provides some insight into personalities, values and morals.
- Afternoon dating reveals more about each person and a more meaningful measure of compatibility can be ascertained.
- Evening dating should be reserved only for serious relationships. Something happens to people when the sun goes down – especially if Barry White's *Love Theme* is playing in the background.

Remember, in the morning, one is more interested in eating bacon and eggs than listening to Barry White. Start a relationship with a "morning" attitude and the flesh will probably not get into a lot of trouble. Single people need parameters when it comes to dating to avoid blemishing their reputations and integrity. Wisdom and caution should be the hallmark of a relationship that is in the early phase. If the morning date works, then the relationship can slowly progress. Don't be blind-sided, naive, vulnerable, or stupid.

I've never heard a couple say, "We waited too long and took it slow." However, I've heard a number of couples say, "We went too fast and rushed the relationship" with regret and remorse.

KEY TRUTH

Keep the relationship holy, respectful, and pure. Allow leadership, such as pastors, to offer advice and be fully cognizant that the church would never abuse anyone's freedom to date. Church pastors and leadership are not going to dictate every aspect of the relationship, but we may know something about one or both of the parties involved that needs to be discussed. Do not date every single and unattached person—use discretion. Include married couples and mature friends as accountability partners and for group dating. Listen to the advice of mature people that know you and that can speak into your relationship. Make your relationship accountable to someone other than each other.

Secrecy or Confidentiality

There have been many instances where a person had knowledge of damaging information that should have been shared with leadership. However, the person was unable to discern when to speak and when to remain silent. Do not make promises of secrecy; particularly when it has been determined that the matter has ramifications that will impact the ministry. In other words, someone says to you, "I'm going to tell you a secret, but you can't tell anyone." That promise can't be made until one hears the information. The enemy can come and cause catastrophic events to take place within the church. There are some cases where common sense dictates that disclosure must be made. Examples include information about a crime, abuse, and certain sinful practices. Silence could cause unnecessary damage to the future of a person or to the ministry. Having information that could be potentially harmful to the ministry must be disclosed. Each one of us has a responsibility to be proactive and appropriately disclose private information to leadership to protect our church.

The demarcation can be difficult to identify between gossiping and releasing pertinent information. When unsure, take the information to leadership, not to the members. The burden of responsibility is shifted to leadership, the shepherds of the flock, to analyze the facts and render an assessment. Consider the consequences of non-disclosure which can be damaging to the church; it could even become a lawsuit against the church. Keep in mind, the church is family and half of the church could be wiped out if something goes wrong. The individual who initially disclosed the information may be angry or disappointed; nevertheless, care enough to tell the truth and intercede to avert possible disaster. Any form of abuse or misuse – as well as potential embarrassment, loss of reputation, damage and harm to people's lives – must be disclosed in an effort to protect at all costs.

KEY TRUTH

Tell the person sharing the information that a promise of secrecy cannot be made. Inform the pastoral staff as soon as possible. Releasing significant and potentially harmful information to leadership is not gossiping if information goes upward rather than downward.

Disputes Between Members

First Corinthians describes the protocol in mediating and resolving disputes:

> Dare any of you, having a matter against another, go to law before the unrighteous, and not before the saints? Do you not know that the saints will judge the world? And if the world will be judged by you, are you unworthy to judge the smallest matters? (1 Corinthians 6:1-2)

A dispute between church members arising from a contract or agreement should be handled by the parties without involving the church. If a resolution cannot be reached prior to initiating legal action, an appointment should be made with the church office for mediation counseling. The church will act as a neutral party and attempt to establish the facts of the case and facilitate resolution. Furthermore, it is not a good witness to the world when Christians bicker and argue and react as the world does with excessive and spurious litigation. Every reasonable attempt must be made to achieve resolution in accordance with biblical standards. However, the Bible also states that if peace cannot be achieved, move on.

Once the church has fulfilled its obligation in providing neutrality and mediation the parties may have the matter adjudicated by the courts. Inevitably, one party will prevail, and one will lose. The losing party, as well as the winning party, must be mature and walk in forgiveness and peace. Very rarely will both parties stay in the church, which is very sad and unfortunate especially since we are supposed to be Christians.

If something is said within the ministry that requires clarification – perhaps dealing with vision, integrity, the heart of the ministry or direction – go to the horse's mouth to get an answer. Do not become involved in a dispute. Do not let anyone use the church, the pastor's name, or any staff person's name flippantly to condone something that is inconsistent with the church's vision or reputation. Use wisdom to determine whether the pastor made the statement or if an opinion is being given. If the remark is incongruent with what is commonly accepted as a truth about the church, a member has the right to pick up the phone, call the office and ask for direction. Otherwise, there is a chance of people becoming offended and leaving the church because the devil used someone to influence others – and the pastor did not have anything to do with it. Unfortunately, I have witnessed the replay of this scenario on too many occasions. The pastor never said or did anything or what he said was taken out of context, and people drew their own conclusions. It's unfortunate when people leave the church because of something that was supposedly said yet not verified instead of going to the church leadership or pastor. Many good people have left a church when they didn't have to because of a bad sheep sharing bad information. We seem to be quick to talk *about* each other rather than have the maturity to talk *to* each other.

KEY TRUTH

The two parties should pray about the situation and then meet to review their conflict before getting others involved. After prayer, if a resolution is not reached, perhaps there is a third impartial party, e.g. a trusted and respected Christian, who can help sort through the differences and focus on bringing resolution to the conflict. Also, don't be so quick to leave the church on one source of information. Don't make someone else's offense yours. Don't make someone's misinterpretation of your offense you perspective.

Proper Dress and Etiquette

We should always be dressed in proper attire; however, special attention must be directed to clothing that is suitable for church. I am not saying that we should not wear jeans or shorts. I am referring to the fact that our attire should be appropriate and respectful. Both Peter and Timothy addressed this area of contention.

> *Do not let your adornment be merely outward – arranging the hair, wearing gold or putting on fine apparel.* (1 Peter 3:3)

> *In like manner also, see that the women adorn themselves in modest apparel, with propriety and moderation, not with braided hair or gold or pearls or costly clothing, but, which is proper for women professing godliness, with good works.* (1 Timothy 2:9-10)

In Romans 14:21, the Apostle Paul brings further clarification and definition to this issue by teaching, *It is good neither to eat meat nor drink wine nor do anything by which your brother stumbles or is offended or is made weak.*

Women, in particular, must respect the church enough to avoid wearing short skirts and low-cut blouses, see-through clothing, very tight revealing outfits, and should always wear undergarments. Thank God women have legs and cleavage, but women must refrain from being disrespectful and revealing too much. They must be aware of how clothing fits. Clothing that is too tight or too short is not proper attire. Remember, not all men in church are delivered. Many are still in the process. They are looking at the shapes and curves of women who wear revealing clothing walking down the aisle and are having difficulty worshipping God or focusing on the pastor who is preaching the gospel. Many women may respond that men are consumed by lust and demons, and they need to be delivered. A mature Christian woman who is a sister in the faith will modify her dress and be ready to minister or be a blessing to a man, not a temptation or hindrance to his faith.

While attending Bible College, a situation occurred that, in my opinion, illustrates the effect an inappropriately clad person can have and how we can cause others to stumble. A sixty-year-old man went to the dean and asked for help. He indicated he felt horrible and God was dealing with him. His problem was a very young, beautiful woman who sat next to him in class. Every time she sat down, her dress went up her legs in a very revealing way. The man said he was trying to learn about God and hear His voice, but he could not resist the temptation and inevitably would turn and stare in the woman's direction.

We must all be fully aware that we can cause others to stumble with our appearance, attitudes, behaviors, and addictions. We want people in church and outside of church to be drawn to Jesus rather than to us. Dress nice, be fashionable, look beautiful and as attractive as you want. Just use wisdom and discretion.

Keep in mind that pulpit etiquette is essential when serving in the choir, band or performing arts. It's amazing how many women, who serve in these ministries, seem to be completely oblivious to their attire – revealing four inches of abdominal flesh or three inches of cleavage! It may not be appropriate for a male pastor or man in leadership to correct a women's apparel, but mature women in the church may be assigned to this task. Maturity levels will determine the outcome – either the woman will be offended or she will receive correction and modify her dress.

Additional Guidelines

Always respect protocol and pulpit etiquette. If you are asked to speak in front of the congregation, do not abuse the privilege either in dress, attitude, behavior, or words. A one-minute testimony is not the opportunity of a lifetime for fifteen minutes of fame. Anyone who violates pulpit etiquette will not, in all likelihood, be afforded the opportunity again. People need to be a blessing and learn to submit to leadership's authority. God honors self-respect and respect for the church. You should always submit to whatever was asked of you – whether it pertains to subject matter, themes, timelines or expression of Holy Spirit. Always honor the house by not bringing a new interpretation or revelation you've gotten when preaching in someone else's pulpit. This could cause confusion to the hearer.

Rules for proper attire also apply to men. Anything revealing or tempting could be viewed as offensive.

Please allow me to share a true story with you. A woman once requested that I pray for her. She stated that she sang in the choir and that one of the men who assisted the women down from the stage would touch her hand as he helped her down. She continued by saying she was single and believing for a husband, but she truly enjoyed the touch of that man's hand. As I considered my conversation with this woman, I suddenly realized that the enemy was using this single woman to stimulate her thoughts in a direction privileged only to a married woman. This all from the simple and innocent act of hand touching. This woman was being honest. She needed strength from the Lord to fight against fleshly thoughts. It would never occur to me that something so seemingly innocent could be the source of temptation for anyone.

KEY TRUTH

Select attire that is not distracting. Ensure that the Jesus in you is being enhanced and not the flesh on you. How will the world know that we are Christians if we look and act no differently from the world? Again, this is not necessarily about fashionable clothing but revealing clothing—showing too much skin. Also, respect the pulpit etiquette or don't accept the invitation to speak. Always view the pulpit as a privilege, not a right.

Christian Duties

It is important to exemplify Christ in all that we do. Our personal conduct must be compatible with our Christian duties. The Bible clearly lists "our duties" as believers. The following is a set of guidelines for Christians:

- Be a witness of Jesus Christ by sharing your faith
- Practice the disciplines of study, prayer, worship, stewardship, and service
- Be faithful in church attendance and tithes
- Live a life that honors commitment to family
- Treat all persons with equal respect and concern as beloved children of God
- Maintain a healthy balance in your personal life. This includes relaxation, rejuvenation, and renewal of emotional and physical self. Sleep, exercise, eating properly
- Free yourself of worry, fear and jealousy
- Refrain from abusive, addictive, or exploitative behavior and seek to overcome such behavior
- Be a faithful steward of God's gifts by managing time, talents, and financial resources responsibly and generously
- Accept responsibility for all incurred debts
- Refrain from gossip and abusive speech
- Maintain an attitude of repentance, humility, and forgiveness while being responsive to God's reconciling will

KEY TRUTH

Let's not be Christians who just believe in Jesus. A Christian is not to be a consumer who just takes and receives, but actively distributes, gives and shares. Don't just go to church; be the church. Don't wear the cross but live the cross.

CHAPTER 4

CHURCH CONDUCT

Bondservants, be obedient to those who are your masters according to the flesh, with fear and trembling, in sincerity of heart, as to Christ; not with eyeservice, as menpleasers, but as bondservants of Christ, doing the will of God from the heart. (Ephesians 6:5-6)

Joining a Church

Anyone who is seriously considering joining a church should be responding solely to the voice of God. Join a church because God is leading, speaking, or guiding you. This act must not be undertaken capriciously or impulsively. Seek God and do not succumb to influence exerted by emotions, feelings, family or friends. There are some who join a particular church because the church is part of a family tradition. For example, the family has attended the church for years; however, the church has been in the same location for two hundred years, but there is little to no growth, fruit, vision or excitement in that church. Be led and guided by

God in making this decision. Spend quality time in prayer and research like you do before a large purchase or marriage.

What about the senior pastor of the church under consideration? What criteria apply in assessing him or her as the church leader? Please understand that there is no pastor who is perfect; however, it is important that he or she be a person who walks in integrity with the Word of God, is visible and exemplifies Christ-like character. There are preachers who do a lot of shouting and are superb orators, but their marriages are at risk and their children are out of control. Be very careful when making the decision to join a church solely based on the outward emotions you see the pastor demonstrate over the pulpit. Remember, the spirit of that pastor will be transferred to his followers. So, it would behoove you to look for a pastor with exemplary character.

The devil is always looking for an open door, and when he finds an area of weakness, he not only will attack the pastor but will go after the sheep as well. For example, a pastor who is contemplating divorce and engaging in flirtatious behavior has opened himself up for demonic spirits to control him in areas of infidelity, lust, divorce, and abandonment of his family. This pastor and his life are out of order and in violation of God's protocol. Look to God for guidance and be aware of any lack of integrity in leadership. Remember, you are looking for a pastor to shepherd you, not just a good preacher.

Therefore by their fruits you will know them.
(Matthew 7:20)

A growing church, where members are being ministered to and fed, will bear fruit. Why would a person choose to join a church that has been stagnant for fifty years with only thirty members? There are some who do and will blatantly assert that the church is awesome because they share a powerful time in the Holy Spirit speaking in tongues and prophesies. Excuse me, but I am now going to be bold and blunt: People who make these statements are naïve and ignorant in the things of God. Churches with minimal or no growth generally are unable to attract large numbers of people who make intelligent, informed choices. These individuals can see through the charade of a stagnant church upon entering the door. A church that does not bear fruit will neither challenge nor affect positive change in its members. They ask the "why" question: Why aren't these churches growing? I'm not against a church that's small in number but don't dismiss the facts. Are there salvations, outreach, evangelism, effective vision, and growth in people's lives?

I do concede, there are always exceptions to any situation. One of the few situations where I can completely understand a person attending a church bearing no fruit is to fulfill a God-given assignment to lead in that church. In this scenario, the church is receptive to this individual because they have been praying for someone to come and help lead and assist the ministry. Under these circumstances, obedience to God takes precedence.

> Look to God for guidance and be aware of any lack of integrity in leadership.

Look for both church and personal growth. Some people have been in a church for years, yet they have failed to thrive. The absence of growth may not be completely attributable to the church. Each individual must assume personal responsibility and institute corrective action. Ponder this question: Is there any manipulation, intimidation, lack of humility, abuse, misuse or extremism?

To avoid joining the wrong church, open your heart and honestly assess and answer each of the following questions:

- Does the new church have a godly pastor who believes in and preaches the uncompromised Word of God?
- Does the church operate with integrity?
- Is the church focused on growth, bearing fruit, vision, balance, holiness, and financial stability?
- Is there an evangelistic and soul-winning ministry or program?
- Is there strong praise and worship?
- Does the church offer a discipleship program?
- Are people growing?
- Is prayer a priority?
- Is there freedom of the Holy Spirit and His Gifts?
- Is the church bearing fruit?
- Is there a vision?
- Is there balance within the ministry—whole gospel, Bible preached and diversity? of subjects?
- Do leadership and the church walk in holiness?

- Are there excellent youth and children's ministries?
- Is there a healthy environment that supports and promotes godly family values?
- Does the church reach out to the community?
- Are biblical values, marriage integrity, and wholesome family values modeled by the pastor?
- Does the church display good stewardship and financial integrity?
- Does the church have a board that the pastor submits to?

KEY TRUTH

Evaluate the church under consideration for membership. Use the above list to make an informed decision.

"Style" versus "Principle"

Each of us has our own unique style, preferences, passions, likes, and dislikes that may be linked to our backgrounds, environmental factors and experiences. We do not leave these preferences outside the door when we enter church; moreover, our experiences with former pastors, congregations, or denominations also shape our church preferences or the lens through which we judge. All of these factors influence our decisions on whether we love the praise and worship style or are receptive to the pastor's preaching style. When joining a new church, expect to be challenged and stretched out of the comfort zone acquired at your old church home. Things will be different, but do not fall into the web of "style" related issues.

When someone gets caught up in the style trap, he will find fault or dislike most things. Glaring problems such as the pastor's speech pattern or teaching style will extinguish any possibility of successfully transitioning to the new church.

Exercise caution and do not get caught up in style preferences, or issues of style will develop into major issues. Major on the majors; resist the temptation to major on the minors. Do not look for fault... the new pastor speaks too slowly... he speaks too rapidly... the choir sings too loudly or too softly. As long as the pastor and the church are glorifying God, be thankful for what God is doing.

ALFC is a great church, but anyone seeking to be offended will be offended. We are a multicultural, multi-generational and multi-diverse church. Everything in the church may not reflect the personal preferences, interests or passions of everyone; however, because of the diverse backgrounds of people represented, we make every effort to make everyone feel at home by providing a versatile and balanced program.

We must all learn to celebrate diversity and clearly differentiate between style and principle. Diversity of race, culture, education, socioeconomic status, gender and marital status are present in the church just as in society. There are those who will work with people from different cultural and ethnic backgrounds but will not worship in a multicultural church. Preferences, prejudice or bigotry? I believe that if a church is in a multicultural community then the demographics of the church should mirror the community. Pastors limit themselves when they reach out to specific ethnic groups alone. Rainbows of people are in heaven.

In communities where there is one dominant ethnic group, local churches should establish outreach programs that open the door for the church and the community to interface and break down the walls that separate them. The diversity of a church will impact the style, but be willing to receive the message, understand the vision, and listen to God's Word, even if the style is outside the realm of your preference. Celebrate diversity.

People share common characteristics related to new experiences, relationships and material things. In the beginning, people love their church, their spouse or new car until the novelty wears off. As time passes, they begin to neglect the thing they once cherished because it becomes familiar. They focus on the faults of their spouse, begin to neglect their car and become critical of their church. Please remember the style preference may not be the issue when new to a church, but may raise its ugly head after the honeymoon period. Be mindful that style issues are frivolous and based on preferences, but principle issues should be seriously considered. Do not leave a church just because the style of the church is not a perfect match with personal preferences.

Matters of principle are legitimate basis for concern. If the pastor is not glorifying God, then there is a principle issue. Principle issues include violation of the Word or doctrinal principles. Carefully categorize and separate questions of style and principle. To illustrate further, consider: Is the problem with the church's music related to the sound (a style issue) or with the message (a principle issue)? Is it (how) something was said (style) or (what) was said (principle)? "Amazing Grace" is a powerfully beautiful song whether sung in a contemporary or traditional style…so let's just sing and enjoy the song! Mature Christians will recognize that there are different gifts and God uses everyone differently. Chew the hay and spit out the sticks!

Verify that what is being done in the church is in accordance with God's Word and is not in violation of the Word. It is important to determine and honestly assess whether personal disputes, differences and frustrations are based on "style" or "principle." For example, if a church begins to make changes to reach more people with the salvation message, implement cost saving measures or enact protocols to improve production, let's be mature to understand the heart of the matter rather than allow offense to take root.

KEY TRUTH

The derivation of any particular style is based on innumerable factors. Styles are subjective and not necessarily principle driven or based. Be flexible when adapting to the environment where God has called you. Do not make an issue of something that is merely a stylistic difference.

Remember, the "style" that the pastor chooses is the one that is most effective for the church. People who are not mature are easily moved by many things such as the look of the stage, paint color, whether or not the choir wears robes, the new check-in system, the sound being too loud or too soft, the length of the service, and the use of different leaders in the pulpit. If the Word of God, the Holy Spirit, and the message of salvation are still present and has not changed, isn't that what's important?

Leaving the Church

If the decision is made to leave a church, ministry protocol suggests that the decision be communicated to the church by letter, email, telephone, or in person. The appropriate method will depend upon an individual's level of involvement in the ministry or personal relationship with the pastor. Communication conveys respect, mutual understanding and facilitates an orderly transfer to a new church. No one should just get up and leave. It would not be acceptable on your job or in your home.

For those who were minimally involved in the church, a personal appointment is not necessary; a letter, phone call, or email will suffice. Those who were involved in leadership should make a personal appointment and share the reasons for leaving the church. Do everything in a decent and orderly manner. An exit that is respectful and loving is the spirit that will be carried into the next season.

God will grow a church in two ways:

1. He brings people to the church.
2. He removes people for various reasons.

It is God's way of "pruning" the church just as we prune a tree. I am always amazed at the number of parallels between nature and human experiences; perhaps that is why Jesus used nature and human experiences in so many of His parables. When a tree is growing, it annually sprouts new branches and leaves. In the winter, the branches must be pruned to make room for the new. There are those who cannot adapt or are perpetually frustrated in a church and need to pray for God to lead them to another church where they can find peace. It is all part of the pruning process. It is called backdoor revival. Of course, there are those who should pray through their emotional frustration and stay.

I believe that if a church is growing, healthy and fruitful, then a significant percentage of the people who are called by God to that church will remain. The church will continue to flourish, minister to the needs, and bear fruit. However, there will be a small percentage that God has placed in a church for a season of healing and instruction or ministry duties. God may require some people to do a work in another church. These people account for those who may leave the church.

Sometimes people leave their church for job related issues, relocation, illness or travel distance. Notifying the church helps the ministry to be able to care for the flock by understanding the reasons for the move. Remember, we are family and nobody just stops coming or leaves home without notification. No one simply stops showing up to his job without notification, a request for a transfer, and first meeting with management. How much more for those who are in Christ Jesus? Of course, issues of integrity, character, or immorality would obviously justify leaving.

KEY TRUTH

Never hurt or damage the ministry when leaving. Disparaging remarks should never be made about the pastor or ministry. Refrain from leaving the church impulsively, emotionally, or under someone else's influence. If God called you to a particular church, then He will be the One to release you. Listen only to Him! Learn to stay planted where God has called you; don't be so easily uprooted.

Reasons Not to Leave a Church to Join Another Church

We need to stop the tumbleweed, church hopping, whirlwind of unhappy saints in their tracks. Are you leaving the church because you feel that all of your needs are not being met? In truth, what church can? That is God's job. Are you there to give or just receive? What is your history or track record when it comes to church? Furthermore, consider the following:

1. If you are leaving because you are hurt or offended, consider: Is this thing a mountain or a molehill; petty or serious? The church is like family. Who doesn't occasionally get upset or disappointed? Are you perfect? Just questions to consider.

2. If you are leaving because you were corrected or challenged by God's Word or leadership, consider: How was it done? Why was it done? Why were you coming to church? Were you possibly guilty of anything? Just questions to consider.

3. If you are not in agreement with everything, consider: Are you seeing the big picture, or is it just your opinion? Is that a reason to stop or quit? Is more being accomplished that is good, great or godly in the church compared to your complaint? Just questions to consider.

4. Is someone's opinion, gossip or personal feelings influencing your decision to leave when in reality you may feel different? Just a question to consider.

5. Have you gone to the church leadership or pastor to question or seek clarity regarding the issue that is motivating you to leave? Just a question to consider.

6. Are you calling something "God" when it is not God leading you? Are you saying, "God is telling me to leave," or "It's a new season,' but it's really an offense, unforgiveness or some other issue? Just questions to consider.

God will not ask you to leave a church without telling you where your next church will be. You do not sell your natural house without knowing where you are going to live next. This also applies to your church home.

KEY TRUTH

When it is necessary to geographically relocate, consider your spiritual priority of a church home. Call the church administration office for church recommendations in your new home area. If you can, always celebrate and speak highly of your old church. Don't recruit people to follow you to your new church. The church is Jesus' body and His bride.

Called to Ministry

If God directs someone to start his or her own ministry, protocol requires that leadership be informed of the calling. In addition, those who join a church and feel they have been called to full-time ministry should also share this information with leadership.

> *And we urge you, brethren, to recognize those who labor among you, and are over you in the Lord and admonish you.* (1 Thessalonians 5:12)

We must respect God and God's people by not causing confusion and division. We must respect church leaders by scheduling a meeting and sharing what God has put in our hearts; then prayer and guidance can be provided for the direction and understanding of the church as it relates to your calling. We want the pastor's blessing and covering.

When the decision is made to leave a church because a calling has been placed on one's heart, it is inappropriate for this person to solicit church members via handouts, verbal invitation, social media or any other means unless approved by leadership. I always tell people to obey the 30-Minute Rule – do not start another church within thirty minutes traveling distance of the former church. Why would God raise you up to go down the street and start another church like the one you just left? God is not the author of confusion. We don't want the sheep to be confused and wander so boundaries are expected.

In the business world, we would never dream of working for an employer for twenty years and then go down the block to open the same business. Secular employers often execute contracts with anti-competition clauses to avoid this situation. Be godly and in order when called to start a ministry. Respect the former church that loved you, blessed you and provided guidance. We don't want to cause the pastor and home church any burdens by our decision.

Anyone who is approached to follow someone who leaves the church to start his or her own ministry has a responsibility and obligation to respond to this type of solicitation for what it is: inappropriate and out of order. This information should be shared with leadership to protect, and out of respect for the pastor and the home church.

I have, on occasion, shared with the congregation that if they hear someone is leaving our church to start their own church, and I have not informed my leaders and the membership that an individual is leaving, it may be assumed that there is no covering or support for that individual's decision to start a church. Some pastors will instruct members not to associate with an individual who leaves on bad terms. I believe that directive is ungodly and should not be condoned. However, if the individual who is leaving the church behaved destructively and hurt members in the church, then the pastor has discretion to warn leadership and the congregation.

There is a proper and godly way to leave a church. If you have a calling referred to as "being sent"; if you have been a blessing to your church, and have discussed with leadership your intent, meet the requirements of starting a church, and you are in good standing; then you are brought before the church, presented, acknowledged, prayed for and sent. If someone says they are called to start a church and are not presented to the congregation, it is usually a sign of the person's failure to follow protocol or the church leadership isn't in agreement or fully informed. Members of the church should be able to interpret this action as improper. If they weren't presented and "sent" maybe there's something that's unknown. True, godly pastors want to protect their flock as well as love people. This is sometimes difficult when proper protocol is not followed. A pastor has to use wisdom and watch his words when he explains the reason someone is leaving. It's much easier to explain when the person is being honored.

A member who ministers outside the church should notify church leadership for accountability, covering, and prayer so the church leadership can also be in agreement and this will avoid confusion.

KEY TRUTH

Permit leadership to pray, counsel, and direct during a transitional season. Be wise when entering and leaving the ministry. The devil wants to bring division through error. Pray about everything and proceed with caution. When coming before your pastor, are you asking him for direction and counsel? Or have you already made your decision and only want to make him aware of your plans? Those are two different perspectives – asking or telling.

Chapter 5

RESPONSIBILITIES TO THE CHURCH AND MEMBERS

But speaking the truth in love, may grow up in all things into Him who is the head—Christ—from whom the whole body, joined and knit together by what every joint supplies, according to the effective working by which every part does its share, causes growth of the body for the edifying of itself in love. (Ephesians 4:15-16)

Lending, Giving and Borrowing

A pastor, with whom I have a longstanding relationship, shared that his wife had been ill, and they were in debt with medical bills. He asked if our church would help him. I prayed about his request, and I decided that we could help him. His request actually answered one of my own prayers that had been placed in my heart – that ALFC would be positioned where we could help other people in fulfilling the work of the Lord; financially assist people with genuine needs and hardships.

> *But this I say: He who sows sparingly will also reap sparingly, and he who sows bountifully will also reap bountifully.* (2 Corinthians 9:6)

One of the many reasons our church is sowing seed or giving is because we are believing God to pay off debt. This is not chump change! I must ensure that our church sows an abundance of seed to reap a bountiful harvest at harvest time. I never want to be in the position where God admonishes us because we failed, as a church, to respond to the opportunity He offered us to sow seed, but instead chose to hold onto our little pennies!

It is within every Christian's nature to give and be generous. However, when one is unable to give, falling under condemnation is not proper. When a request is made for a loan and the request is denied, the heart of both parties will become clear. When money or other requests for support have been denied, anger should not be the response. Do not allow any condemnation from those who are upset because their requests were rejected.

Use wisdom in all situations whether lending, giving, or borrowing. Lending to those when there is no basis for trust or a history of faithfulness can be problematic. Never lend to individuals with reputations for nonpayment or those who have previously taken advantage.

Do not be reluctant to ask questions when someone requests to borrow money or things. It is preferable to make an informed decision; invoke good stewardship over God's blessings. Exercise good judgment and common sense. For example, if someone asks to borrow your car, do not feel compelled to lend your car when it is your sole source of transportation to work.

> *Do not be one of those who shakes hands in a pledge, one of those who is a surety for debts; if you have nothing with which to pay, why should he take away your bed from under you?* (Proverbs 22:26-27)

Do not place your name, reputation, welfare, well-being and family on the line for someone else. Of course, the situation may be different when asked to co-sign for a member of the immediate family or a trusted close friend. Always remember, however, such an arrangement can jeopardize credit standings and the relationship if things don't go as planned. When people want to borrow money from me, and I don't have peace about it, I always say, "For the sake of our friendship, let's not even go there." Not everyone within the church is a developed, fully mature Christian.

> *Owe no one anything except to love one another, for he who loves another has fulfilled the law.* (Romans 13:8)

There are babies who don't know how to take care of anything. They love Jesus, and they are on their way to heaven. But when it comes to material things, they're lazy and can't be trusted. Just because they can sing and preach, does not mean they have their house in order. They may look anointed and spiritual – that doesn't mean they are that way in all areas of their lives.

> Use wisdom in all situations whether lending, giving, or borrowing.

NEVER, EVER give money you cannot afford to give or money that should be used to pay a debt or bills. I don't care what preacher, prophet, or evangelist he may be. If he tells you to bring him an offering, and you don't have it to give, do not go into debt and pay 21% for ten years on your credit card so he can walk out of there with a big offering. Consider the consequence... getting stuck paying for the credit card bill for the next several years. God knows our hearts. If there is faith enough to give, that minister better have faith to receive it, no matter how small – remember the widow's mite.

Giving or lending your mortgage or other bill money creates a poor impression. How many of us can call our creditors and say, "I can't pay you this month because I have lent a sister in the church some money. Would you please have mercy on me? By the way, we are having church services on Sunday morning. Please come. I want to invite you." That scenario gives God a bad name. God expects us to honor our commitments, first, before He would ever put it on our hearts to lend someone anything. That's not God; this behavior can be attributed to an emotional response of the enemy. God wants us to first pay our commitments and honor our priorities.

KEY TRUTH

Use the same natural and spiritual precautions that would be employed outside of the church. Refer the person to the pastor over the care ministry for financial counseling. Never borrow or lend church property without approval. Watch for people who borrow money. Notice them, direct them to leadership, and let leadership know about them and their need. Sometimes, as it relates to private functions, rental fees can be issued because of upkeep and responsibilities on church property. Facilities can change because of needs, vision and demand. Understanding and patience are required. Remember the church's property is a part of God's house. We are to protect and watch over God's house.

Use of Church Property and Facilities

Pastors and church leaders may request and arrange for the use of buildings and rooms within a church for ministry or department-related meetings or events. Use of facilities and services by members or groups should always be made far in advance.

The removal of church property and the use of the church logo or name is prohibited without express consent and approval by the designated church leader.

KEY TRUTH

A member should submit a request to the church administration to use church property or facilities. Then, the member should confirm the request a minimum of five business days prior to the scheduled event. The confirmed request ensures that everything has been done decently and in order. Do not assume it is acceptable to borrow or use church facilities or property without prior approval. Remember to always ask first!

Monies

Never give money – tithes, offerings, or payments – to anyone except those in authority. Money should never be collected within a department on the church property without prior approval. There are times when people have needs within the church, but there is a system and approval process that enables the church to provide covering. The church can gather pertinent information to avoid hurting innocent people. No one should ever independently solicit donations to make a car or mortgage payment for himself or herself or a third party. There may be a history of repetitive borrowing to cover basic needs; money given to these individuals will be a quick fix. What is not common knowledge is that the same person made the same solicitation six times last year. The world would never lend money to someone with that history.

Anyone who is approached to collect money for a third party should decline participation. Verify if approval was obtained from the church administration. Also, confirm the name of the administrator. If you discover that no prior approval was given, advise the individual that the collection of money has not been approved and this action violates church policy. Leadership must be apprised of such solicitations for money. An evaluation by leadership will either confirm or fail to legitimize that the need exists. Furthermore, no one should count money alone, retrieve money alone, nor take money home. Always have accountability for your protection.

KEY TRUTH

Never initiate or participate in the collection of money unless duly authorized by church administration. Make leadership aware of requests to collect money. Respect people's vision. Leadership permission and direction are all obtainable when guidelines are met. Although a need may be urgent, it doesn't mean someone has the right to ask people to give to that need. Keeps everything ethical, integral, and respectful.

Soliciting and Conducting Business Affairs within the Church

In Proverbs 16:20, the Word instructs, He who heeds the word wisely will find good, and whoever trusts in the Lord, happy is he. Furthermore, in Romans 14:16, we are instructed, Therefore don't let your good be evil spoken of. Never use personal position or influence within the church for advertisement or soliciting. The church grounds must be kept sacred, neutral, and non-threatening to others and should not be used for selling products, conducting business transactions, distributing promotional materials or recruiting for personal business ventures.

There are churches that are business-oriented, as evidenced by the presence of ministries for entrepreneurs. These churches want their members, who are business owners, to succeed. In a controlled environment, the church supports them via business expos and ministries where every participant is treated equally and no specific enterprise is favored. It is inappropriate for those who use the trunk of their cars to conduct business to barrage and inundate church members with flyers and product samples. People come to church for God, not for Mary Kay, candy bars and Tupperware. On the other hand, it is a different matter if a business owner is approached and the other party initiates a conversation. Walking in wisdom becomes the basic principle when people solicit a business owner on the church property. Give the individual a business card or contact information and have him or her contact you at home or at the office. When approached, be mindful of the church setting. Pyramid schemes where people are recruiting churchgoers to join multi-level organizations are to be avoided because this can be a sensitive subject when it comes to investments, employment and sales. These are sensitive subjects that have caused a lot of irreparable damage in the church. Additionally, guard against people who have a business idea to help the church but that also benefits them financially.

KEY TRUTH

Remember why we are on the church grounds… to advance God's Kingdom, not ours. Conduct only His business on church grounds and during church hours.

Donations, Gifts and Purchases

God and the church appreciate the desire to bless His house and His people, but we must remember that God is a God of order. Should you desire to bless His house, it is proper protocol to notify the church administration office to get direction to ensure that donations, gifts, or purchases are aligned with the church's vision. The church has specific policies and procedures that must be followed.

Some people think the church is like the Goodwill and give things to the church they don't want. The gift may be nice, but the church may never use it. Furthermore, if the church has limited space, a warehouse must then be rented to store the donated items resulting in an additional expense to the church. Follow protocol… check with the church administration office to verify church policy on this issue.

I have had people say that they want to donate a car and when one of our staff members inspects the car, he discovers a heap of junk on jacks with no wheels and the engine torn out. It's a faith car because it will take the Lazarus kind of faith to call it back to life. What am I supposed to do with it? I do not have the resources to repair it, nor am I able to speak life into it again like Jesus could. I need something I can work with. Once again, please follow established protocol.

Do not be offended when the church is selective about donations and gifts. A gift will be received with integrity and appreciation when church guidelines are followed. These guidelines will eliminate misunderstandings and hurt feelings. You should never feel that your gifts to the church warrant some kind of entitlement or special treatment. Let's give with no strings attached as if you've given it to Jesus. Do not buy things for an event, activity, outing – such as decorations – and expect reimbursement unless pre-approved.

KEY TRUTH

Speak with the church leadership concerning any plans for the conveyance of a gift. Do not make any purchases that require reimbursement without prior consent and approval.

Contractual Work for the Church or with One Another

Refrain from performing work on church property – paid or voluntary – without approval. If payment is expected, an approved requisition must be granted. This process guarantees protection, safeguards the church against possible liability, and aids in our overall ministry of excellence.

In 1 Timothy 5:18, we learn that "the laborer is worthy of his wages." I have been in ministry a long time and have seen people perform services and then come back and complain that they were never offered remuneration. When I hire someone to do work at the church, I want to know the specific cost, in writing. If there is work to be done on our church property, I solicit bids. Membership does not act as surety against shoddy work. I want to see some recommendations. A member may be a professional painter, but then when the job is inspected there is paint all over the carpet and all over the baseboards. The "painter" may walk out of there praising the Lord, and now I have to assign three staff members to clean up the mess! We end up having to repaint the walls, while the painter thinks he did a good job! Always inspect the work before final payment is made. This should be stated in the contract before the work begins. Payment disbursements may look like half upfront and half at the end or one-third up front, one-third in the middle and one-third at the end.

Use wisdom when it comes to contracting work with other members. Do not ask for freebies or discounts just because they are our brothers or sisters in the Lord. Maintain the same standard of doing business with both church and non-church members. Recommendations, bonds, and contracts should be expected before closing the transaction. Do not let the fellow church member avoid doing things in an orderly and decent manner by stating, "Well, I am just going to bless you. I will give you a good deal. I will take care of you because we are family." No! Execute an agreement; keep that relationship healthy.

KEY TRUTH

Work with the pastoral or administrative staff member who has the authority to grant permission and issue payment for any contractual, construction, or voluntary work done. When work is being done, paid or volunteer, make sure that the church liability insurance is current and covers volunteers. This will ensure that the church is protected against an unfortunate accident or lawsuit. Keep in mind that a contract may be necessary for volunteers depending on when work is being done, length of assignment, cost of materials, description of work, etc. If you are volunteering your trade to do work for the church and not requiring any payment, treat the job with the utmost integrity and respect as if you were getting paid. Whatever you promised to do and whatever timeline was given or due, God will bless you.

Recruiting Members in the Ministry of Helps

Before approaching or permitting anyone to work within a department, ensure that the prospective applicant has undergone the proper interviews, new membership classes, and applicable training. Follow whatever protocol has been set-up by the church. You never want the church's reputation to be affected.

KEY TRUTH

If someone appears overly eager to work within a department, learn more about that individual. Reputations are so hard to build and can be lost so easily when protocols are violated or ignored.

Quitting a Department or Ministry

When an individual decides to leave a ministry or department, closely examine the fruitfulness of the department and evaluate the following:

- How does one know when a season, assignment, or duty has ended within a department or ministry?
- Have you been instrumental in implementing changes resulting in positive results?
- Have you notified leadership of your decision to move on, and will you speak well of your time of service?
- Is there anyone to replace you, or will the department cease to exist?
- What is the next God-given assignment?
- If there is a personality problem with another fellow worker, have you given leadership a chance to rectify?

Following protocol in this area will prevent offense which results in murmuring, complaining, strife and division. We are blessed here at ALFC to have a healthy church; nevertheless, I am just sowing seed for the future. Preventative maintenance is taking place, so when the healthy sheep see an unhealthy sheep, this book will be available to share and provide guidance.

KEY TRUTH

Pray about the situation; then, seek confirmation and guidance from the pastor over the department or ministry to ensure the will of God for your life. Respect the church authority that God has gifted to you. If you are leaving to go to another church to help them in the same field of ministry, please notify leadership early on. Seek guidance for they may know something you don't know. They may also want to celebrate with you as you're released into your new season. Moving to another department or ministry within the church because you would like to experience a new ministry or opportunity is encouraged.

CHAPTER 6

ACCOUNTABILITY IN RELATIONSHIPS

Walk in wisdom toward those who are outside, redeeming the time. (Colossians 4:5)

BE A HEALTHY and mature Christian. It's amazing how quickly people disconnect from their home church when they don't like something or something doesn't go according to their expectations. People carry their issues and problems into the church and never really "settle" or "plant" or "get healed of the past". Problems exist in their marriage, finances, or with their kids and they blame the church for not being there for them. They allow past pain to rise up and rob them from where God has called them. Too many good people I know have left our church because of something insignificant, petty, and maybe even childish. I know people who can't get along with one individual so they stop coming to church and disconnect from their spiritual family and the place God called them to.

KEY TRUTH

Ask yourself if there are any blind spots—vulnerable areas that you are susceptible to and that you carry into other areas. What do you need to be healed, whole and delivered from?

Called to Be a Friend or Friendly?

We must walk in wisdom with those who lack moral fiber or have a criminal background. Understand that not all Christians within the church are delivered or developed in character. Some may lack integrity, ethics, righteousness, and holiness. I realize that we all want to believe the best of every person. However, exercise discretion before disseminating any personal information or forging new relationships.

We must be careful not to inadvertently share something with someone that can be used to attack our character, integrity, or family. Exercise common sense and always protect your home. Be loving, friendly, cordial, and peaceful, but cautious. Do not invite questionable people into your home to meet the family. Again, walk in wisdom toward those who are outside the body of Christ.

Those who are single, in particular, must exercise wisdom. Do not solicit individuals to make home repairs or mentor young family members. Contact the ministry for assistance and referral information. Avoid probable disaster. Furthermore, do not blame the church or the pastor when you make a personal decision to operate outside the confines of ministry protocol.

KEY TRUTH

Always be led by the Holy Spirit in every area of your life. Remember, we are not called to serve everyone so use discernment and wisdom in your daily decision-making process. Don't ignore the warning signs and be naive because they all call themselves Christians.

Confronting

Christians seem to find confronting one another distasteful and operate very poorly in this area; however, God's Word in Matthew 18:15-17 provides the framework for confrontation: Moreover if your brother sins against you, go and tell him his fault between you and him alone. If he hears you, you have gained a brother. Pay close attention to the word, "alone."

> Due to our disobedience to God's protocol, there frequently continues to be no resolution.

Do not include the pastor or anyone else, yet. If someone behaved inappropriately toward you, your spouse or children, it may be necessary to confront that person in accordance with the guidelines in the gospel of Matthew.

The Word of God is perfect and has a system in place for confrontation: But if he will not hear, take with you one or two more, that by the mouth of two or three witnesses every word may be established. Witnesses will then be present to verify the truth of the matter asserted. Moreover, the presence of witnesses will serve to diffuse a potentially explosive situation.

If the matter is not resolved, and if he refuses to hear them, tell it to the church – but if he refuses even to hear the church let him be like a heathen and a tax collector. Powerful! It is very clear; these verses provide the protocol we should all follow to protect ourselves. In our disobedience to God's protocol, there frequently continues to be no resolution in the church today.

If someone's actions or deeds offend me, according to the Bible, I can confront that person. Please understand me... I am not endorsing unbridled judgment of other people's lives. I am saying that within the context of a friendship if something is done or said that offends and hurts the relationship, there is an absolute right to share the disappointment and make every attempt to get to the root of the problem. Let's not talk about one another to others but learn to talk to one another. Let's be mature enough to have dialogue to bring a resolution.

We are wrong when we tolerate one another's sin. We are also wrong to hold on to what someone did to us. This results in a lack of accountability and spiritual growth. If both believers are practicing sin, then neither person is holy or righteous enough to confront the other because of his or her own transgression.

There was a time when we expected and accepted correction in love and looked after one another. People no longer want to be corrected and immediately become defensive. This situation is unfortunate because people want to see the anointing and power of God, yet they fail to realize that it is contingent upon living a holy life and how we handle relational breakdowns.

Few of us would be comfortable confronting an usher observed leaving a liquor store every Friday with a six-pack. We need strong, holy men who will admonish and correct in these and similar circumstances. How could it be unclear to anyone why we fail to witness Bible miracles when we ignore and tolerate so much? Why do we have so many once close relationships that have grown distant?

We want to see the power and anointing of God in our church and in our lives. We want to see great unity in the church. We want Him to bring souls to the altar in large numbers, but what are we willing to do to see this happen? We should want to get right with God and stop sinning! Please forgive me if this seems harsh. The question remains, "What are we willing to do for the power and anointing of God to manifest in our church and in our lives?" We can no longer ignore others, gossip about others, or avoid others and not seek restoration.

As brothers and sisters in Christ, we should have healthy relationships in church. Good marriages include accountability and correction. The book of Galatians provides a perfect example of confrontation. Paul confronted Peter about his lifestyle and behavior. As you know, Paul and Peter were both very important and instrumental in the early church; they were what can be termed as "bigwigs." In Galatians 2:11, Paul corrected Peter publicly because Peter's sin could influence others.

As representatives of Christ and His church, we should think about the influence inherent in a leadership role. Christian leaders are to turn away from the world. When a majority of the ushers, choir, and counselors are backsliding, there is no power, no holiness and no growth within that church. No one is willing to admonish or correct and pride becomes a factor. The practices of the world have crept into the church when there is a blatant disregard, reluctance, and reticence to confront individuals with their sin. People are more concerned with their horizontal position in the church rather than their vertical position with God; not offending others while offending God.

When we seek to participate in church leadership, it is imperative that we are never in a position where our veracity can be questioned – raising issues that may require confrontation and correction. For example, when an individual completes an application to be in a leadership position – or assume a paid or unpaid position – in church, it is assumed that the questions are answered truthfully. If consistent tithing is a requirement to hold a leadership position, then respond honestly.

> *Now I urge you, brethren, note those who cause divisions and offenses, contrary to the doctrine which you learned, and avoid them. For those who are such do not serve our Lord Jesus Christ, but their own belly, and by smooth words and flattering speech deceive the hearts of the simple.* (Romans 16:17-18)
>
> *Yet do not count him as an enemy, but admonish him as a brother.* (2 Thessalonians 3:15)

Throughout the Word of God, we see how the church was appropriately disciplined. Today, church leaders avoid discipline for fear they may lose the big tithers, or someone will be offended. The leadership lacks courage and character to confront people who are in sin. Church leadership would rather offend God and quench His spirit than confront and offend people.

The need for discipline in the church is absolute. Unfortunately, there are people who do not want to be disciplined because they are lifted up in pride. They love their church and pastor until they're corrected or confronted. The level of maturity is then revealed as they leave the church. This scenario explains, in part, why there are so many sick and wounded leaders. After they have sinned, they fail to go through the process of restoration before they are appointed to new positions. Some even leave the organization or denomination and start their own ministry. They do not accept correction. Correction is done to restore, not to judge. If one's position is that correction and discipline are acceptable as long as it's someone else that is a sign of inconsistency and immaturity.

When a person repents, then correction is handled in a totally different manner. That individual is ready to be picked up, built up, and restored; however, if defiance is present, the Word tells us that we will be rebuked. An individual may be asked to leave the church, following counseling where he is instructed to desist from murmuring and complaining – particularly if his or her behavior is detrimental to the congregation. When confronting, use the Word to affirm, encourage, and to be factual. Share scriptures to support the circumstance. Admonish with humility and offer solutions. As the person initiating the confrontation, do not assume "a holier than thou attitude." A third party, who has influence with the person being confronted, may need to be present.

KEY TRUTH

Pray before and after the meeting. Some questions one should ask prior to confrontation include:

- Do I have the right attitude?
- Am I being true to God's Word and instructions?
- Do I have all the facts?
- Do I have influence with this person?
- What will the individual's reaction be?
- Is this a good time in this person's life for this type of meeting?

Strictly adhere to the Word of God and His protocol; otherwise, the person's interpretation and perception of the event may be skewed. Every person should be correctable in the church, especially those in a leadership role. A person may say they submit to authority but when correction takes place, often the character of the person is revealed.

Mentoring

There are a myriad of responsibilities inherent in a mentoring relationship. The mentor must have time to give to the relationship and be able to pray and provide guidance.

> *And the things that you have heard from me among many witnesses, commit these to faithful men who will be able to teach others also.* (2 Timothy 2:2)

Paul passed the Word on to faithful men. They, in turn, passed the Word on to other faithful men. Mentoring is spiritual-based. We must pray and ask the Lord to lead us to people who need mentoring.

A good mentor has a broad base of experiences to access and share. Mentors should be caring, loving, and patient. It is crucial that a mentor be a person of integrity and character. Strong believers should connect with young believers and pour their hearts into them while serving as a role model and confidant.

Boundaries must be established to sustain a viable and mutually respectful relationship. Healthy mentors do not control, manipulate or dominate and will direct a person to Jesus and not themselves.

At ALFC, we dedicate babies whose parents are sometimes very young and who bring their friends, who are also very young, to be godparents to their babies. Theoretically, godparents are to be experienced persons who can provide the child with guidance and act as mentors to the parents in raising the child. The sole criterion for being a godparent should not be based on the fact that we are buddies and love to hang out together. Look for mentors who have experience in the area where help is needed. Do not align with mentors who are struggling in the very area where you need mentoring.

God wants us to have mentors to facilitate growth. You may have thirty friends whom you admire, but mentors are a select group of two to five individuals. Take the matter seriously; remember that not all of your friends are mentors. Mentors will hold us accountable, and we must share our weaknesses to be accountable. Do not confuse fellowship situations with accountability groups.

We must accept a basic precept: we need to learn to be accountable to the Word of God. We need someone physically on this earth, besides the Holy Spirit, to whom we can be accountable. The nature of the flesh is to consistently want to do the minimum or test the boundaries.

Mentors give advice and counsel, but they are not in our lives to tell us exactly what to do. Some mentors are going to be in our lives only for a season, while others may be there for a lifetime. I personally advocate that everyone be on both sides as both a "mentor" and "mentee." It is possible to be mentored by someone we have never met in person. Chuck Swindoll could be a mentor through his books, podcast, and radio or television program. Nevertheless, we must always pray and look to God first; He will always be there for us.

KEY TRUTH

There are three rules one should follow when choosing mentors:
- Select mentors who have been where you are going.
- Make sure they are highly disciplined, organized, and obedient to God.
- Be certain you can trust them with your heart and private issues.
- Know if they have mentored others and if they've added value to their lives and growth has occurred as a result of mentoring.
- Listen to their advice. Don't waste their time if you don't want to listen.

CHAPTER 7

LEADERSHIP

Remember those who rule over you, who have spoken the word of God to you, whose faith follow, considering the outcome of their conduct. Obey those who rule over you, and be submissive, for they watch out for your souls, as those who must give account. Let them do so with joy and not with grief, for that would be unprofitable to you. (Hebrews 13:7,17)

Authority and Protocol

The Word of God is replete with recounts related to authority and leaders. Many people are not blessed because they are not submitted to authority. Moses recognized authority and submitted to his father-in-law, Jethro. Moses was very prominent, yet he submitted to Jethro's authority (Exodus 18:13-25). Daniel and Nehemiah provide other examples: Daniel asked permission not to defile himself (Daniel 1:8-14) and Nehemiah asked permission to rebuild the walls (Nehemiah 2:4-5). These individuals asked for the king's permission before they acted. They were men under authority.

There are exceptions where practical needs must be met. It would not be considered usurping authority if assistance was requested from someone else in a position of authority. For example, if a children's church teacher needs supplies and has completed the correct procedures and followed the process but remains unable to procure supplies, it would not be out of order to pursue another avenue to obtain the needed materials. In your church home, you can expect the support of others.

In order for balance to occur, those in authority must also submit to other authority figures in accordance with God's Word. There are checks and balances for those in positions of authority; otherwise who would correct the authority figures? In my opinion, there needs to be more than Jesus and the Word, although Jesus and the Word are the primary sources. I personally need someone here physically in case I am not hearing the Lord or the Word. Although I am the Senior Pastor at ALFC, I have submitted my life to another pastor as my spiritual father. He has the authority to correct me whenever he believes it is appropriate and necessary; we should want to live under the authority of another pastor, church board, spouse, elder or minister, inside and outside our churches. Leaders without authority figures over them to correct them are susceptible to disaster.

Authority figures must earn respect, but they must not demand respect. Titles and positions do not necessarily translate to automatic respect. Respect is earned through love, character, integrity, faithfulness, fruit, and consistency. While an authority figure is following Christ, he is worthy to be followed. Any authority figure who begins living or acting contrary to the Word is not a suitable leader under any circumstances, and it is time to leave that church. 1 Corinthians 11:1 clearly states, "Imitate me, just as I also imitate Christ." The command is unequivocal.

Authority figures must limit their involvement in the lives of others. Do not submit to authority figures that control, manipulate, or dominate lives. The Bible expressly states that pastors are not to lord over their congregations. We do not first belong to the pastors, but to God. Pastors are only stewards and caretakers. There is no need to obtain a pastor's approval, permission, or authorization to conduct personal business. There are pastors who attempt to control every aspect of people's personal lives from what kind of car to buy, what job to take, who to marry… the list is endless and constitutes lordship. Pastors are to shepherd the flock, not lord over them.

> "Imitate me, just as I also imitate Christ." The command is unequivocal.

Respect those who are administrators, directors, and leaders but remember that no one is perfect. The people in these positions are selected because they have our heart and the skills to do what is needed. These individuals support the pastor who cannot be all things to everyone. When someone is referred to a particular person, it is because we believe that the need will be expeditiously met without having to wait several months to meet with the senior pastor.

We honor God by respecting authority figures by praying, supporting and submitting. A rebellious individual who does not recognize or respect authority will usually suffer negative and serious ramifications, consequences and repercussions throughout life until he or she learns to follow God's Word and submit to those God has placed in positions of authority. Being under authority makes you trustworthy and it's God's protection and accountability plan.

KEY TRUTH

Always pray before questioning authority. Be humble, sensitive and mature. Respect them for who they are.

Correcting Leadership in Public

We must always remember that public loyalty produces private leverage. It is inappropriate to correct leadership publicly. Follow protocol if there is a lack of agreement:

- Pray
- If the matter continues to burden your heart, schedule a private meeting where concerns can be shared in love
- Be tactful

In reality, members may not be able to change leadership. The pastor may not believe that change is needed, or the changes that are at the root of the disagreement may be doctrinal and not aligned with the church's vision. The choice becomes plain: either submit to that leadership and continue to pray or move on to another church. Every church has a different culture, vision and style. Understanding this can eliminate frustration and misunderstanding. Each church may handle counseling, funerals, weddings, and hospital visitations differently. The Senior Pastor's travel ministry, how many times he or she is in the pulpit, may be different than what you are used to. Seeking understanding is essential to your fitting in.

KEY TRUTH

Christians are frequently under scrutiny and are representatives of Christ. Settle disagreements in private so that your good will not be spoken of as evil.

Chapter 8

SPIRITUAL MATURITY IN THE GIFTS

How is it then, brethren? Whenever you come together each of you has a psalm, has a teaching, has a tongue, has a revelation, has an interpretation. Let all things be done for edification. If anyone speaks in a tongue, let there be two or at the most three, each in turn, and let one interpret. But if there is no interpreter, let him keep silent in church, and let him speak to himself and to God. Let two or three prophets speak, and let the others judge. But if anything is revealed to another who sits by, let the first keep silent. For you can all prophesy one by one that all may learn and all may be encouraged. And the spirits of the prophets are subject to the prophets. For God is not the author of confusion but of peace, as in all the churches of the saints. (1 Corinthians 14:26-33)

Gifts of the Holy Spirit

The Apostle Paul gives us a clear teaching, carefully outlining the use of the gifts of the Holy Spirit in 1 Corinthians

12, 13 and 14. These chapters instruct us in the protocol of how the gifts should flow – order, guidelines and methods.

It is imperative that we all fully grasp the true meaning of these chapters and verses – with the operative words being order and balance. I am not against the gifts of the Holy Spirit being displayed within the church setting, but there must be protocol in this area as well. It becomes clear that we are never to use the gifts of the Holy Spirit for show, disturbance, distraction, or offense. (To learn about the nine gifts of the Holy Spirit, referring to 1 Corinthians 12.) As 1 Corinthians 14 clearly expresses, there is a way to operate and use the gifts of the Holy Spirit. God, in His Word, commands that everything be done decently and in order. The underlying issue is we must understand and accept that protocol is applicable. Yet, some people feel that if a Holy Spirit gift is being given to them they should be able to go into automatic mode with no regard for their surroundings, church protocol or even God's Word. They have a word to share… now! Confusion could result, and this is not God.

For example, if someone in the congregation feels the Holy Spirit is giving him or her a word in tongue, the Holy Spirit will also give an interpretation or a word of knowledge if there is no interpretation. The Holy Spirit would not make anyone stand up and draw attention to him or herself and disobey the protocol of the house. If He did that, then there would be confusion within the body because people would not know from whom to receive due to the lack of order and confusion. Generally, the pastor in charge or there's a person on the stage leading.

If the Holy Spirit moves an individual to move forward in one of the gifts, the protocol followed at ALFC is to wait until the praise and worship transitions into a moment when the congregation is reflecting on God. This is the perfect time for the person to step forward with the word God has put on his and/or her heart.

For those who feel that the Holy Spirit is impressing upon them to give a word, we suggest that they get the attention of leadership. Let leadership judge the word. Some people do not choose to exercise this option because they feel that they will lose the inspiration of the Holy Spirit. If it is truly the Holy Spirit, He will return or be retained. Please engage in restraint and follow protocol so that the gift can be received rather than confusion.

> Follow protocol so that the gift can be received rather than confusion.

Whether visiting another church or attending your home church, it is crucial that one understands church protocol. A person must be approachable and able to accept correction, if necessary when it comes to the gifts of the Holy Spirit. Even when a person is seeking to be used by God, it is possible to say something that is totally unscriptural. A person may give a word like this: "The Spirit of the Lord is saying to pay off all debts and not tithe." If this word was given at ALFC, the leadership would go to that individual and express appreciation for the zeal but explain that what was said was not scriptural. God specifically tells us to tithe. God is not inconsistent. A person must remain humble and not allow pride to enter when correction is given. It is possible for a person to "miss it" when giving a word, this is neither uncommon nor fatal. Make certain that everything is done decently and in order.

Over the past 34 years, I have had the opportunity to see how people respond when correction is given. People frequently become indignant because they believe this area is so spiritual there could not possibly be any room for correction.

My response is I would never correct the Holy Spirit – that thought would never occur to me. However, I am correcting a person who is flesh and blood and can miss it just like me.

When people become familiar with the church service, congregation, and the leadership, they may say things that are based on common knowledge or things shared among the church family. As an example: If I were to go to lunch with a member, and he shared with me that his back was hurting, and I sensed the Spirit of the Lord wanting to heal him, I might say to him, "The Spirit of the Lord is here, and He wants to heal you right now." Well, I need to make sure this was the Holy Spirit and not just my emotions. God's healing power is readily available; nevertheless, there is a thin line that we must be careful not to cross. We must be absolutely certain we are hearing from God and not just moved by emotions.

I know you can miss the word, because I have missed it. My heart was in the right place, but I was wrong in what I sensed the Lord was telling me. In our church, there were two sisters who so strongly resemble each other that they could be mistaken for twins. I was privy to information about one of them because she had asked me to pray for her husband who was not saved. Well, I was flowing in the Spirit, giving words to people, and encouraging them. I went to one sister and said, "God is telling me to tell you to hold on because your husband is going to get saved." She came up to me afterward and said, "Pastor, I am not married. My sister is married."

See! I thought I was giving the word to the sister who was married and had previously spoken with me. Obviously, that was not the case. I apologized to her and accepted full responsibility for the word that I had given to her.

There are people who refuse to be corrected. They act irresponsibly and will not accept the fact that they were wrong. They may even say, "Well, just deal with that word. I am a prophet. Praise the Lord." No, that attitude is totally unacceptable.

If the word was missed, accept responsibility for that word. We cannot go around telling people that they are going to travel; they need to sell their cars; they must give away their house, or they should marry a particular person. We are out of order when we engage in this type of behavior. Always remember that people who are submitted to the Holy Spirit are willing and able to be corrected.

When sharing a word in tongues by the gifting of the Holy Spirit and having waited a few moments and no one interprets it, it is your responsibility to give the interpretation. If you cannot, then you missed it. Honestly evaluate your personal level of maturity. The word is coupled with responsibility, so if the Holy Spirit gave you the word in tongues, believe me, He will give you the interpretation. He does not want confusion.

If one of the pastors at ALFC has a word in tongues, I will wait to see if the pastor or someone else will interpret it. If no one comes forth, that does not mean they missed it. God could speak to several people with the interpretation, but people can be apprehensive and fearful so they will choose to remain silent. If no one comes forth with an interpretation, I will go to the pastor and say, "You have to step out in faith and deliver the interpretation. I will give you a second, but just move in it." If the response is they are not sure what to say, I will ask the pastor to remain silent the next time.

I have observed super-spiritual people who have a word in tongues but cannot provide an interpretation. Someone needs to go to that person and address the issue. Spiritual balance must be maintained in the church. Moreover, we must all remember when the word is understood, it will edify, uplift, and encourage.

If you are a person who frequently operates in the spirit, make a conscious decision to give other people an opportunity to step out and avoid controlling and manipulating the service. It is not about any one of us individually, but about Him.

In small Bible study meetings, I have observed the same person or persons repeatedly giving a word. Members of the Bible study all know who these people are and frequently defer to those who have been informally designated as those who give a word. We all have the Holy Spirit. People give words differently. It does not matter if a person cannot quote Scripture, is not eloquent, and does not flow like someone else. I may simply say, "The Lord loves you." Whereas someone else will say, "God wants to put His loving arms around you, and He wants to touch the depths of your heart, dry your tears, and feel your pain." If the word is from the Holy Spirit, it will be similar even if the words are not exactly the same. The words used by one are not superior to the other—both were correct and from God.

When someone is operating in the gifts of the Spirit, the word will never challenge leadership. God is not going to use anyone to challenge the leadership publicly. There are babies in the Lord present and correcting in this manner gives the wrong witness.

The gifts of the Spirit are sovereign, yet some people judge or label a church as not being anointed (spirit-filled or spirited) because there are no signs of the gifts of the Spirit flowing in the service. The gifts of the Spirit cannot be turned on and off like a light switch. The gifts of the Holy Spirit are not the only sign of His presence. There are other signs of the Holy Spirit operating within a church. For example: Are people getting saved? Are lives being touched? Is there measurable growth? These things cannot transpire without the presence of the Holy Spirit because He is the agent of the church. This point cannot be reiterated enough… protocol must be followed in all situations. There are no exceptions. The purpose of God's Word is to give us structure, parameters, and boundaries. God gave us the Holy Spirit, the gifts of the Spirit, and His Word to guide us. Abide by His Word in all things.

KEY TRUTH

When visiting another church, first get permission from their leadership to use your gifts. Remember that permission must be granted. If not, they will have difficulty receiving from you, especially if you are correcting them. You may want to wait until after the service to approach the pastor or leadership or send a carefully written letter to share your word with them. When unsure about the timing of giving a word, get the attention of leadership or wait for a more opportune time.

Receiving and Giving Prophecy

I enjoy prophecy, and I believe in the five-fold ministry. 1 Corinthians 14:3 and 32 read, *But he who prophesies speaks edification and exhortation and comfort to men… And the spirits of the prophets are subject to the prophets.* These verses do not refer to the five-fold gifts of a prophet's ministry found in Ephesians, but to the individual who is used in the gifts of the Spirit or who may prophesy. This individual is subject to the correction of the Word of God.

Prophecy is meant to edify, uplift, and encourage the body. The prophecy should confirm what God has already said as well as the Scriptures. A prophecy will reinforce, not violate, the Word of God. Furthermore, prophecy is conditional, based on obedience to God. One cannot expect blessings when there are deviations from the plan, purpose and will of God. When one prophesies to another, the other person has the right to judge the prophecy and the prophet. In one of the five-fold ministry gifts, I believe God gives the prophet greater insight into prophecy so that it always edifies and uplifts the body.

Prior to the "9/11" tragedy, I heard people prophesying we needed to get our finances in order and not get caught up in the system of the world. God's strong message was that His people needed to do whatever necessary to get out of debt. This prophecy was a challenge to the body of Christ. It was not gloom and doom, but a message that served to strengthen and encourage us.

It is important that we exercise judgment, discretion and wisdom when watching or listening to devices, radio, and television. We all know our personal sensitivities and weaknesses. If the uncompromised Word of God is not being shared, refrain from listening or watching. We must be open and pay close attention to the Holy Spirit and follow Him; He will tell us to whom we can listen. The Bible says to take heed what you hear. Not all Christian information and messages are accurate. Use discretion when listening.

It is commonly taught that everyone can prophesy. I agree that when defined as edifying, uplifting, and exhorting, we all share this gift. In contrast, not everyone is a prophet. With that respected office comes privilege and practice. I cannot completely agree that everyone has the ability to publicly give prophetic words. When we use our heavenly language, we control it and do not need the Holy Spirit to come upon us to practice the gift. I do not know if it is possible to stand up and start giving words that affect people's lives without authority, permission, or recognition. Nevertheless, there are those who unequivocally teach that this can happen to a believer. I have personally been down this road and have gone to both ends of the spectrum in my beliefs. I remain undecided on this issue. I am not ambivalent in my belief that deception must be avoided at all costs. Carefully consider the precept being taught—each believer has the ability to spontaneously access another's private life and give them a word from God. I question whether God would grant unrestricted freedom in this arena. Consider the private and sensitive issues. It's understandable if there are areas where correction is necessary.

Someone once publicly gave me a word about my wife Cindy and me. The ministry endorsed that word, but I did not because it was not from God. God is not going to deal with my private and personal business publicly. The matter had nothing to do with sin, but with an issue we were dealing with in the privacy of our bedroom. I will just leave it at that! The person said, in the presence of others, that God was going to bless us in this area of our sex life… I could not believe my ears! This was a very specific word about a private issue that no one knew about; I immediately recognized that this person was operating in a familiar spirit, but certainly not the Holy Spirit. The Holy Spirit would not embarrass my wife or me in this way. Everyone else was caught up in the emotion and shouting, "Hallelujah." We need to stop and truly evaluate why we are shouting "Hallelujah! Praise the Lord." Are we shouting about the word or just being emotional? I could not and would not receive the word that was being given.

Prophecy confirms, not directs your life. A prophecy is not a direct command; it will, however, confirm what God has already told someone. For example, a person who is considering marriage may be offered a prophecy supporting a marriage… "to get that woman (or man) to the altar." If God has not communicated that word to you personally – and you know there are issues with the person you are considering marrying – the word is not from God. The word would have confirmed God's previous messages to you about this person. Just smile and say, "thank you," but do not go home and believe it was God with the specific instruction to get that person to the altar.

Prophecy will never violate the Word of God. An individual once approached me and shared that there was a member of our church who was experiencing financial difficulties. This person further informed me that he had a word from God to release this person from tithing due to their financial challenges. My facial expression immediately transformed from a loving pastor as I had to correct this person and express, in no uncertain terms, that the word shared was not scriptural; therefore, it could not be from God! Remember a prophecy is not greater than the Bible and will never contradict God's Word.

Prophecies are not for dependence, but for inspiration. There are some who are so dependent on prophecies to survive that they feel compelled to go see the prophet on the East Coast and then follow him to Texas or anywhere else he may be. They fail to rely on prayer or the Bible but need a word when faced with challenges or decisions. Why would God use someone else to direct our lives when He wants us to be dependent on Him? Pray and rely on God, not a prophet or his prophecy.

Prophecy is based on our obedience. If I have a word for someone who is living in sin, the word given may not come to pass. When we avoid the course God has specifically laid for us, the word is subject to change. God has no obligation in a life of sin.

Prophecy should come from a trusted vessel. There are some who prophesy that God is going to bless others financially, but they cannot pay their own bills! Others attempt to direct marriages, but are in strife with their own mates! We must exercise common sense and caution before allowing any and everyone to prophesy over our lives.

Please do not misunderstand me. I am not advocating that we must be perfect before we can give a word or prophesy into someone's life, but we had better be whole and healthy. If we are not, it is not our season. If God is going to use us in this arena, then our lives must exemplify credibility and be without impunity. We do not want to cause more offenses than blessings in the body of Christ.

Prophecy is subject to judgment. We read in 1 Corinthians 14:32, And the spirits of the prophets are subject to the prophets. If I am given a prophecy, I want to be able to judge it. If someone says that he or she is a prophet, then the prophecy will come to pass.

Be wary of people who stare as if in a trance and proclaim, "Oh, glory! What is this I see? In thirty days, your wife will conceive and in nine months she will bear a child." If the wife does not conceive and does not bear a child, then who missed it? It undoubtedly was not God. I prefer, for those who say they are sensing something from God, first ask permission to speak into someone's life. God is not going to force a prophecy or a word upon us. He has given us free will to choose for ourselves. We must be careful when people say, "God said." A true gift from God is going to draw attention to Jesus and not to self.

On occasion, God will use pastors to speak into someone's life, and it will be very authoritative, but even then there is always the possibility of making a mistake. If this happens frequently, despite a sincere heart, God will provide guidance. Always evaluate and judge how and what is prophesied. When any one of us is wrong about a prophecy, be humble and repent. Take responsibility for the gift.

Conclusion

This book has been a work in progress for several years beginning with the first idea impressed upon me by the Lord. The principles from beginning to end are based on the Word of God given to the Body of Christ as the rules of law to govern our lives successfully.

As I considered the laws in God's Word, I realized that throughout history no civilized society has survived without law and order. The secular world does not openly espouse God as its governing authority; nevertheless, governments also impose laws for the purpose of maintaining order.

The God-centered principles outlined from Genesis to Revelation have been given to God's people to teach us about human relationships. People must learn to live in harmony and apply principles of fairness, equity, justice, integrity, honesty and trust as taught in the Word of God.

It is my prayer that *Ministry Protocol* will be used as a guide to pastors, leadership, support staff, volunteers, and the Body of Christ to avert unnecessary misunderstanding and confusion among God's people. I hope that *Ministry Protocol* will be woven into the fabric of every person, family and church leadership that constitute the root of the local church. *Ministry Protocol* can also be instrumental to church organizations who desire to prosper by following the principles in God's Word to do things decently and in order.

My final thought is I believe our witness for Jesus, through our lifestyles, actions, decisions, choices, and words is the greatest accomplishment, purpose and fulfillment for Christians. Knowing what, how, when, where and why to do things as Christians require the wisdom, knowledge, and understanding of conduct and the lifestyle of ministry within the church environment.

Many wonderful Christians will live their lives in error, falsehood and deception because of lack of knowledge, improper modeling, and willful intentions. My prayer is that the foolishness, embarrassment, and immaturity within the church will be openly discussed. I pray that a true, godly spirit of communication will take place to liberate the Body of Christ with the truths found in God's Word so that our witness as believers will speak volumes to the world of the Great God we serve.

KEY TRUTH

So walk in wisdom, be a balanced Christian and don't flaunt spirituality. Be mature believers.

That we should no longer be children tossed to and fro... (Ephesians 4:14)

Who has bewitched you that you shall not obey the truth... (Galatians 3:1)

Stand fast in the liberty by which Christ has made us free... (Galatians 5:1)

Lest Satan should take advantage of us; for we are not ignorant of his devices. (2 Corinthians 2:11)

Test all things, prove all things so you will have victory, joy and understanding in the things of God. (1 Thessalonians 5:21)

For precept must be upon precept, precept upon precept. Line upon line, line upon line, here a little, there a little. (Isaiah 28:10)

ABOUT THE AUTHOR

IN 1994, PASTOR Diego and his wife Cindy founded Abundant Living Family Church (ALFC), which began with twelve people. Abundant Living Family Church has three weekend services and a Wednesday night Fresh Start Bible Study. The weekly attendance is over 6,000, and God continues to increase with new members. The church's vision is clear, "To seek the lost, teach the found, and send the disciples."

Once an aspiring professional triathlete, Pastor Diego was diagnosed with stage 4 kidney cancer in 2008. His doctor indicated that no one he knew with this disease had ever lived more than six years. A miraculous journey of faith led to his complete healing and the birth of the Health Initiative Revolution. What also increased was Pastor Diego's faith, knowledge, and understanding of how to better steward our physical bodies to accomplish all that God has for each one of us.

Pastor Diego is committed to ministering to the whole man – spiritually, physically, financially, and emotionally –

with priorities focused on family, youth, and children. His style is simple, allowing the hearing to easily identify and apply God's Word to his personal life.

Author Contact

Abundant Living Family Church
10900 Civic Center Drive
Rancho Cucamonga, CA 91730
(909) 987-7110 Phone
(909) 484-5288 Fax
www.alfcrancho.church